ARTFULLY MODERN
Richard Mishaan

ARTFULLY MODERN
Richard Mishaan

WRITTEN WITH JUDITH NASATIR

THE MONACELLI PRESS

TABLE OF CONTENTS

INTRODUCTION 7

ALL ABOUT ART 12
MASTER CLASS 14
MODERN MASTERY 32

LIVE WITH WHAT YOU LOVE 52
ALL ABOUT YVES 54
ARTISTS IN RESIDENCE 60

HOME SWEET HOTEL 84
MIDCENTURY MODERN 86
HAUTE HOTEL 98
LA CASA EN EL CALLEJON 122

IT'S ALL IN THE MIX 164
SINCERELY YOURS 166
DINNER AT EIGHT 178
OVER THE TOP 198

THE EVOLVING HOUSE 218
HOME IS WHERE THE ART IS 221

ACKNOWLEDGMENTS 270

INTRODUCTION "White. A blank page or canvas. The challenge: bring order to the whole. Through design. Composition. Tension. Balance. Light. And harmony." Those are the opening words of *Sunday in the Park with George*, Stephen Sondheim's miraculous musical about art and the artist—and my favorite show of all time. Whenever I am asked to describe what I do as an interior designer, his brilliant, brief statement of the creative process comes immediately to mind. Not only does he capture in a mere twenty-one words what many of us find difficult to articulate at all, he communicates a complex idea in a very immediate way.

I face that blank page—and the challenge of reordering the home—with each new project. Where do I start? Inspiration comes from everywhere and anywhere, from the strangest object to the most perfect one, from the oddest space to the most sublime. Composition, tension, balance, light, and harmony? For me they are always in play—consciously or subconsciously.

The design process can seem abstract, but it always begins and ends with the client. My job is to understand who my clients are and how they live. This means I study human nature, behavior, and relationships. I sometimes even jokingly refer to myself as an anthropologist. When I interview clients, I gather as much information as possible about their particular lifestyle, needs, passions, and aspirations. I want to understand how everyone who coexists under the same roof functions—parents as well as children. With that information, I start figuring out how to fill the blank canvas—to create environments that will sustain, support, and embrace a specific individual or family. A major component of comfort is an architectural background that can adapt gracefully to the additions of furniture and objects that occur naturally over time for all of us, collectors or not.

Our personal chronology at a given moment in time affects the types of homes we choose to inhabit and the decorating decisions we make. This is true from our first apartment after college to a primary family residence for a growing brood to a weekend retreat. In each scenario, space planning, furniture, fabrics, objects, and artwork vary. Young families need their homes to be safe, playful, and child-friendly. As baby-proofing knobs and corner guards disappear and Fisher-Price "decorative objects" in primary colors take over every room, as rambunctious children emerge into somewhat sophisticated—or at least opinionated—teenagers, our rooms evolve. When the children become young adults and fly the nest, we embark on yet another of life's phases and our homes evolve yet again. I am currently living this truth with my own family. As a designer, I instinctively recognize it in others.

Good design is directed, progressive, and flexible enough to embrace accident and serendipity. Certain clear external clues—and some more subtle—inform a designer about what steps to take in the beginning. Location is the single most important consideration. That means topography, climate, culture, history, local vernaculars and traditions, and so on. Time of life is an important second factor. A third is individual taste. These parameters form the foundation of all design decisions to come. Any decision made that's out of context will simply look and feel wrong. The proper context always feels right. There's still plenty of room for flexibility and individual expression within that basic framework that allows for style preferences and the clients' vision.

Collectors in particular need special design attention. An urge to collect comes from a passion—or, in cases like mine, it may also be genetic. My mother and her mother have been avid art collectors. She drew me into it over the years by lending me spectacular pieces, saying: "I've got this and I want you to take care of it because I have no more room." To me, inherited pieces that may have been acquired fifty years earlier give a room soul. Regardless of the assessed value, a piece may be priceless to me because it reminds me of my heritage, my friendships, and so on. While the things that we collectors treasure may grow in monetary value over time—and we always hope that they will—the true value of our collections has little to do with dollar signs. Their real value lies in reminding us of the time we made an original discovery, in the thrill of the hunt (which can take years), and in living with the things that we love for as long as we can. One of my great joys as a designer is in helping clients discover a passion for collecting. I want to introduce them to the fun and excitement of finding and acquiring beautiful things. I want to watch them develop the hunger for more knowledge and the next piece, and see them revel in the real pride that accompanies the creation of a great collection over time.

Everything about art fascinates me: the artists themselves, the materials they use, the intention, the imagination, the execution, the evolution of taste, the shifting perceptions of the market, and above all, the joy, excitement, beauty, and richness that it brings to our everyday lives. That captivation is what I hope to share with my clients, and I will happily work tirelessly to make their homes just as artful and livable as possible.

I am the kind of art collector who cannot stop. I am constantly learning something new and at the same time am trying to stay ahead of, or at least on top of, change. The deeper we delve into a period, region, or specific artist and the more we understand about it, the greater the chance of recognizing something unique—or a good deal—before others do. Some people are satisfied by surrounding themselves with just a few lovely things, not a comprehensive collection. That's fine by me, but those who do collect seem to seek me out. It's at that point that the adventure begins for both parties. It's wonderful to have any type of deep passion. It simply adds a new dimension to life.

As I see it, my role as a designer is to give context to collections and to help them have kinship with modern life. How? With tricks of the trade. Contrast, punctuation, grammar, tone, and vocabulary are what writers use to bring order and interest, rhythm and surprise to the worlds they create with words. Those same kinds of tools exist in interior design, but designers speak in furnishings and objects, color and material palettes, textures, and choice and placement of artwork. Think of ill-conceived design as one long, dull, run-on sentence. All things of a certain visual value belong together, can coexist together, or can make the visual experience more interesting. The acquisition and placement of a single piece causes a ripple effect in the visual and emotional landscape of a room. My task is to find a way to bring order to the whole.

Making people comfortable in their homes and expressing who they are—that challenge inspires me with each project. It's about a level of detail, a level of design, a level of art—yet the owner's hand must be visible in all of it, too. I want that blank page or canvas to look like a portrait of the client in the end. A good room is like a pointillist painting viewed from afar: the picture is composed of separate brush strokes that work together in perfect harmony.

ALL ABOUT ART While the majority of us want to live with remembrances of things past, we want to do so in surroundings that suit our lives today. That's actually a lot less Proustian than it sounds—we simply treasure inherited pieces and wish eventually to give them to our children. We also cherish our antique, vintage, and collectible furniture, objects, and artwork for the inherent beauty and personal history each piece represents, regardless of its place in the cultural or chronological spectrum. But interiors must be contextually appropriate and true to our time to be comfortable. That's one reason why period rooms, once a staple of American decorating, are such a rarity these days. Understanding history and tradition is still critical if you're to showcase captivating beauty and invention well in an interior, however. One-of-a-kind pieces pose my biggest—and most captivating—challenge as a designer, architect, and collector.

Choose one particular century to start from and bring it into today by inserting cutting-edge art of the moment.

A mix of centuries is fascinating. Each piece, each era, each century enhances and comments on the other. Giving context to a client's artwork and belongings is the most satisfying part of my job.

I saw Yves Saint Laurent's Paris living room early on in my career, and it has continued to inspire me since. It contained an unbelievable mix of cultures, styles, and periods—from Napoleon III to Art Deco to the ancient world. Rare chairs by Pierre Chareau. A tabouret by Pierre Legrain. Art by Léger, Matisse, de Chirico, Modigliani, Klee, and Les Lalanne. He blended them with African pieces, Orientalist overtones, and crucifixes! It was the best of everything. That room clarified what I was just beginning to suspect through my own first forays into collecting: there are no rules, you don't need permission to blend periods, and quality pieces always work together. Over time, acquisitions create a tapestry. If you love something, it's not only right—it's perfect.

MASTER CLASS Creating a show house room is an exercise in imagination. Sometimes you have to invent a situation and characters, almost like writing a play. Sometimes the house hands ideas to you on a silver platter, as the 2011 Kips Bay Decorator Show House did for me. That year it occupied a neo-Federalist townhouse that once belonged to John Hay "Jock" Whitney—financier, publisher, sportsman, art collector, tastemaker, and onetime ambassador to the United Kingdom. I was assigned the ballroom-sized living room—all 60-by-40-feet of it. I was thrilled. It was a fantastic opportunity. My mission was, clearly, to bring the world of the Whitneys into the present day.

As excited as I was, we were in a recovering economy and I did not want to be insensitive by simply creating an absurdity of riches—even though it would have been contextually appropriate! On my way home from High Point Market, I mentioned how torn I was to Margaret Russell, the editor-in-chief of *Architectural Digest*, and a mentor and friend of over twenty years. Over coffee at the airport's Dunkin' Donuts, I asked her advice. People who

visit Kips Bay want to see magic and find inspiration. I didn't want to disappoint them. She, insightful as ever, replied: "Make it a master class—a real education." Today's Whitneys would place less emphasis on classicism than their predecessors. To my mind, they would be more like Guggenheims: interested in the avant-garde and the new, but with a deep understanding of the past. Design today is about celebrating the freedom to stretch convention and to mix periods and provenances.

When the architecture of a room has historical relevance, as this one did, I always believe it should be respected. Painting this room's classical elements an ivory color created a soft, welcoming background—a true context for living. Two spectacularly beautiful English mirrors—in the room since the Whitneys' time—gave me a starting point for selecting furniture, objects, and art. If you look closely, you'll see a direct line of descendants from the French master of marquetry André Charles Boulle and *menuisier*

LEFT: A powder-coated metal chair designed for Bolier & Company's outdoor collection, upholstered in a red-and-white tiger print and juxtaposed against a traditional fireplace mantel, proves that all objects with design integrity go well together.
PREVIOUS PAGES: Fernando Botero's study for *Mona Lisa* updates the room's English gilt mirrors. The Moroccan rug is similar to one in Yves Saint Laurent's living room, and continues the geometric patterning introduced on the walls to the floor in a subtly different way. A Murano glass chandelier adds a 1940s flavor to the mix of periods present. OVERLEAF, RIGHT: A tribal table, the essence of simplicity, looks particularly modern in the context of a room that contains many elaborately detailed elements.

Georges Jacob to Jean-Michel Frank and Jules Leleu to today's most talented furniture designers like Mattia Bonetti, André Dubreuil, and Jean-Bérenger de Nattes. Art Deco takes inspiration from eighteenth-century furniture and twenty-first century furniture modernizes Art Deco motifs.

Each of the pieces selected for this room references both tradition and modernity, art and craft, the avant-garde and the rediscovered. The navy blue-lacquered Leleu table at the entrance has a truly classical form, made modern by its balance and lacquer. The André Arbus rug is a gorgeous original with a pattern that is definitively from the 1940s, but is also a recognizable update of border shapes used in Savonneries. Collectible furniture and masterful art elevated each other's presence simultaneously and enticed the eye. Visitors were captivated with learning about each piece, so it was gratifying to not only create a successful room, but to delight and to teach at once.

RIGHT: A built-in niche—formerly a dumbwaiter—becomes a bookshelf holding a still life of objects unified by color and form. The André Dubreuil hurricanes were purchased twenty years ago but continue to look modern in this context. PREVIOUS PAGES: An original André Arbus rug dates to the 1940s. The thin silhouette of Mattia Bonetti's whimsical, gilded, hand-hammered metal chairs relates well to the rug's graphic border.

RIGHT: Mercury-glass
mushrooms are one of several
pieces in the room by
contemporary artist Rob Wynne.
OVERLEAF, LEFT: Niki de Saint
Phalle's *Nana* is a bolt of
pure happiness, plus it mediates
the scale of a room with 17-foot
ceilings. OVERLEAF, RIGHT: A
rare 1930s Rothschild commode
is topped by a Sophia Vari
sculpture based on Art Deco
forms. Damien Hirst's diamond-
dusted butterfly kaleidoscope
prints hang above.

Royal Crown Derby's classic
Imari-patterned porcelain has a
kaleidoscopic, boldly colorful
pattern that brings timeless
decorative ornament to a
tabletop. Flower and fruit
arrangements add to the visual
abundance. Contemporary
stemware and flatware
make the tableau modern.

30

MODERN MASTERY Upon the birth of our second child, my wife and I set out to find a new apartment that was close to Central Park—my wife is an athlete and an ardent supporter of the Central Park Conservancy—and, most important, that it be convenient to schools. This apartment in Carnegie Hill met most of our criteria, so we traded the space and 12-foot ceilings of our Upper West Side place for great views, park proximity, and 9½-foot ceilings. What a lesson. The change in dimensional context made me see my art much differently.

When we bought the apartment, it still had a lot of intact original ornamental plasterwork. For the first few years, I felt obliged to be respectful of it. At a certain point, though, I found the excess of classical detail oppressive. I removed a layer or two of it and then finished it in white lacquer, which acted nicely like a palate cleanser. Today the envelope is ornate, yet with the detail silhouetted by lacquer, it feels

modern. I also swapped the living room's very traditional fireplace for one with simple, modern lines. After those two interventions, the apartment started to come together stylistically.

Our foyer features 360 degrees of artwork and contains furniture from around the world and many different eras. Whenever I bring a new piece into that entry space, what inhabits the hall table, what surrounds it, what pieces play off one another—and why—changes. Adding and editing the foyer makes me feel a little like I've freshened the entire apartment.

Perhaps because I have roots in Colombia, I love the vibrancy that color adds to a living space. To temper it for a New York location, however, I use a muted or neutral background and introduce color through fabric here and there and through art, like the Manolo

RIGHT: A foyer filled with art welcomes visitors with a burst of vibrancy. A brilliantly colored painting by Kenny Scharf dominates one wall; Guy de Rougemont's rare Archipelago table holds an ever-evolving mix of small sculptures and objects, which here includes a philosopher's stone rendered in metal by Chinese sculptor Zhan Wang and my first KAWS, given to me by my son.
PREVIOUS PAGES: In the living room, an Alexander Calder stabile cozies up to a sixteenth-century Italian gilded mirror.

Valdés pieces that make my living room so cheerful. The living room has a sense of collectedness that could only come from acquiring pieces over years and years. My Giacometti coffee table, for example, I bought over fifteen years ago. The gilded, carved mirror is a memento of a trip to Italy taken twenty-five years ago. The console I had custom made in sharkskin and Macassar ebony, in the style of Jean Dunand. With its Baccarat crystal decanters and Christofle silver accessories, the old-fashioned setup for the bar reminds me comfortingly of my parents' home. The far side of the living room houses more treasures: a pair of Leleu lacquered chairs and coffee table; a limited-edition chair by Eric Schmitt that I carried in my shop, Homer; a Goudji crystal bowl; a spectacular painting by Manolo Valdés; a Lalique vase; and tables from Maison Jansen.

RIGHT: Fernando Botero's *La Putica* is on permanent loan—from my parents. The same artist's marble still life was a wedding present from them, and sits atop a shagreen-topped console I designed after the style of Jean Dunand. OVERLEAF, LEFT: A Miguel Berrocal puzzle torso catches the light from an innovative stacked-slat lamp, Homefire by Salomé de Fontainieu. OVERLEAF, RIGHT: A Guy de Rougemont side table sits in front of the updated fireplace. PREVIOUS PAGES: The Donald Baechlers over the sofa and a Niki de Saint Phalle *Nana* sculpture bring vibrant color into an otherwise neutral-based room.

LEFT: A red-lacquered Jules Leleu table was a serendipitous find. The metal sculpture on the pedestal in the corner and the painting at right are by Manolo Valdés. RIGHT: The table setting is my Chinoiserie design for Lenox China. A Lalanne mouse adds whimsy. OVERLEAF, LEFT: A Barry Flanagan sculpture rests on a Leleu coffee table also graced by other decorative objects with clear or crystalline features. OVERLEAF, RIGHT: A watercolor by Elizabeth Peyton draws the eye to a vignette of decorative objects in celadon hues.

I have a fascination with arranging objects and artwork on shelves along with books, so for my library I designed a bookshelf with metal plates that disperse the light evenly. Opposite are a Leleu table and chairs—I feel lucky to be able to call it our everyday dining area.

I've never thought of working in one particular style; I love to mix it up too much. The spaces that interest me most are those that are dynamic and evolving. Every time I find and bring home a new piece, it redefines the entire area around it, changing the way my eye catches on things and helping me to look at and appreciate familiar things in a fresh way. This apartment has changed dramatically over time—and will continue to do so in the future.

RIGHT: A Fornasetti rug's serpentine motif leads sinuously down a hallway that ends at an Iván Navarro light sculpture.
OVERLEAF, LEFT: A David Hockney Gregory portrait brings brilliant color to the library, where we eat many family meals.
OVERLEAF, RIGHT: Giò Ponti flatware and Royal Copenhagen china form an unexpected partnership on the table.
PREVIOUS PAGES, LEFT: Studio Job's whimsical, fantastical Taj Mahal table is a fitting display space for mementos of my wife's travels in Thailand, Cambodia, and Africa.

LIVE WITH WHAT YOU LOVE I have always been a collector. Once I discover an artist, period, or specific type of object, I research, explore, and covet owning a piece almost obsessively. In the end I decide on what to acquire based on inner passion alone—not price speculation, not trendiness. To my mind rooms that are filled with objects the collector truly loves are the most successful.

Art and interior design are flip sides of the same coin. Each involves issues of balance, composition, color, and harmony. What really makes great art or design, though, is not so much what is present as what is not. The Japanese call the "spaces in between" *ma*. It's invisible when the work is finally shown, but instinctively detected when a room's proportions are right and it feels curated, not merely overstuffed. The same goes for color—in painting as well as interior design. Just how much hue creates significant, memorable intensity and presence?

The variability of the design process keeps me interested and curious. There's a formal progression to every project, yet the nature of that process differs with each client. Defining visually what makes someone tick is almost like rendering a therapy session in three dimensions. I know I've been successful when people are surrounded by things they truly love—and that includes a wide variety of styles and objects. When I go into the home of a person who does not work in a visually creative industry, my task as a designer is usually to bring formal order to their pieces. When I work with artists, however, that order is almost always in place so the process evolves from an entirely different perspective— we exchange ideas and learn from each other and about each other's aesthetic preferences. Thus we both become each other's student. In the end, as the Chinese proverb says, the teacher does appear when the student is ready to learn.

ALL ABOUT YVES Successful design comes from an ability to execute a vision, but that vision itself emerges from a very artistic place. That's why show houses are so important to a designer's development. They give us the freedom to get back to our most creative selves and serve as a great laboratory of possibilities. When *Hamptons Cottages & Gardens* invited me to participate in its inaugural Holiday House Hamptons, I was thrilled. The theme: festivals. So why not a birthday ode to Yves Klein, and a table set just for him?

Dining rooms are the one space in the house where we always want drama. The decor should help to entertain guests and stimulate all the senses. For that, color is essential. People tend to shy away from strong color, but it can certainly define a mood. Klein's signature, electrifying shade of cobalt blue gave me a great opportunity to explore how to balance such intensity with other elements in the room so as to dissipate the tonal resonance and make the room feel serene—now that's a lesson in design.

RIGHT: To fill this show house room with great art, we created it ourselves. Klein's *Winged Victory* would have been perfect for this room, so my staff and I made it first, then re-created his *Venus di Milo* while we were at it. Could-be Cy Twomblys and a faux Richard Serra helped us appreciate the difficulty of creating modern art and give the room an edgy vibe. PREVIOUS PAGE AND OVERLEAF: Yves Klein's stunning, saturated blue sets the scene for a fantasia on the theme of his birthday. Carefully selected accents include glass, flatware, and china from Lenox, plus wall sconces and ceiling fixtures of my own design.

ARTISTS IN RESIDENCE It's an extraordinary privilege to have the opportunity to work with artists as clients. They of course have a very specific way of looking at life, and their homes must express what makes them feel comfortable, reveal their color sensibility, and include space for displaying their own work. Visually acute people make me approach interior design with a different process, and I love that. For starters, it's guaranteed that their residence already reflects a truly personal sense of style, which absolutely broadens my horizons. They have tableaux, vignettes, quirky collections—and a unique way of displaying them. There's no better way to learn. The challenge for me as a designer is to do something very light-handed for artist clients, yet noticeable enough so that change and a professional touch is apparent.

In this home, two artists live and work together in a space that's constantly changing by virtue of what each does. This couple is certainly a case of opposites attracting. He's a warmhearted Texan and a world-famous painter with a

passion for nature, taxidermy, arcane subjects, and eccentric objects. She's a sophisticated British beauty and potter; a collector of textiles, antique pottery, and furniture; a lover of English and French country styles and everything those terms connote. Their one complaint about their enormous SoHo loft? When they are home together with their son, it feels gigantic and not at all cozy.

The apartment is a perfect artist's studio: L-shaped with 20-foot ceilings, ornate plasterwork, gilded details, and your typical structural columns. Brilliant—and problematic. She disliked having the entire interior viewable from the entry. He loved its openness. He thought it was fabulous to be able to set up tables down the middle of the room to host large dinner parties. She thought it felt like a cavern and hated the way noise traveled from space to space. To satisfy them both, we created huge screens that they could position at will—and that also proved to be great backdrops for his artwork.

LEFT: Although the pieces are of different provenance, curves on a console's legs unite it in sensibility with those of a ribbon ornament atop an eighteenth-century French gilded mirror. Atop the console is a *nature morte* composition featuring a taxidermied crocodile and animal skulls. PREVIOUS PAGES: Custom 17-foot screens serve as both room dividers and additional display space for art in the SoHo loft. A John Alexander jungle painting rests on the narrow ledge at right.

RIGHT: In the dining room, a camelback sofa-cum-banquette pulls up to an oval table. A John Alexander landscape of a foxglove meadow hangs above. A red-and-white ikat fabric from the owner's textile collection upholsters one of the dining chairs. OVERLEAF: In the den, a neoclassical Biedermeier daybed faces a contemporary metal-and-glass coffee table of my own design to establish a theme of eclecticism that continues with fabrics of various periods and provenances.

They already had many wonderful pieces, so the focus was on context instead of content. We repositioned furniture pieces or altered them slightly to make them that much more unique. The console, for example, now creates a proper sense of entrance—but it was originally floating elsewhere around the apartment. She had a rickety old sofa and a table that she wasn't particularly fond of, but that I didn't want to discard. We reupholstered the sofa and positioned it like a banquette behind the table to create a cozy little nook for reading the paper and intimate family dinners.

It's an understatement to say that this couple is not into fancy living or pretension, so simplicity throughout was our rule. Her textile collection became intrinsic to the decoration, almost subconsciously. We used what she already had as upholstery fabric, pillows, and throws. The variety proved to be incredibly harmonious. We upholstered all her furniture to refresh it, then added subtle custom details—piping, trims, welting—for definition and understated elegance.

RIGHT: A book-filled bedroom is the expansive SoHo loft's coziest space. The rolling library ladder provides additional display space for the wife's textile collection, including a Navajo throw. PREVIOUS PAGES: A display of the wife's pottery, arranged to draw attention to contrasting forms, colors, and textures.

The den coalesced around a Biedermeier daybed, which we made an accent piece by surrounding it with very modern designs. Bookshelves nearby were full of wonderful things—and wild plants. I lined up the shelving to divide the dining room from the den and put the flora in planters to give it a sense of formality. What pulls the room together, paradoxically, are the varied colors and patterns of her textiles.

We laughed together at the arrangement of bedrooms—the son has the room that would ordinarily be considered the master. Chalk up one more artistic subversion of the norm! The parents' bedroom is tiny, book-lined, nurturing, and a place to nest. I think it looks like the Cotswolds, and it's somehow very Zen. Unlike most couples, including my wife and myself, these two have the freedom to live in the entire apartment, which continues to change all the time.

RIGHT: A sample of John Alexander's work, which relies primarily on traditional media such as watercolors, oils on canvas, pastels, and monotypes. PREVIOUS PAGES, LEFT: Art permeates the loft, including its kitchen. PREVIOUS PAGES, RIGHT: A long, windowed interior hallway leads to the bedrooms and terminates at a classic artist's studio.

HOME SWEET HOTEL I've noticed something ironic evolving over the course of the past decade or so: private clients now request specific hotel comforts in their primary and secondary homes while hotels, on the other hand, want their suites to feel as homey as possible.

Guests at four-and-five-star hotels tend to fall in love with how practical and luxurious the rooms are and how seamlessly they integrate the latest technology— they have everything from pop-up outlets on bedside tables to cleverly-placed USB ports and TVs that glow discreetly from behind mirrored walls. Many of our residential clients ask us to incorporate those kinds of features into their homes now that most everyone sees a house as a live/work environment.

Hoteliers, on the other hand, focus on providing their guests with a memorable experience, but today's rooms must be dynamic. Executives need suites that function just like a corner office—complete connectivity, screens for A/V presentations, and a conference table. Families want that same table to convert to a breakfast area and they want the screen for watching cartoons. A small hotel in Provence, for example, will also try to create the ambience of a private home so that guests feel they're in an incredibly quaint B&B.

Crossing the hospitality/home design divide gives me a chance to push boundaries. The residential design aesthetic exists to set a tone, and it requires more restraint than a commercial space. That said, homes today already embrace both the functional and the experiential aspects of hospitality design to some degree. Dining rooms, for instance, certainly benefit from heightened drama: as dining out has evolved into entertainment, sensational dining rooms with a clubby air come to feel right at home. Conversely, restaurants now often try to recreate the atmosphere of a cool downtown apartment. Working on both allows me to cross-pollinate in fun ways.

MIDCENTURY MODERN A client and good friend who also happens to be an exceptionally design-savvy executive for a major Italian fashion company commissioned us to design his one-bedroom pied-à-terre on the Upper East Side. He had a very clear vision of the kind of chic, midcentury American aesthetic he wanted it to represent: *Mad Men* meets *La Dolce Vita* meets The Mercer Hotel. He also knew that when he stayed there, he wanted to feel like he was in a five-star boutique hotel. This apartment has all that, but because it's a private residence it can also express his masculine, minimalist style.

Given that this client splits his time between Milan and New York, the theme of hotel living made complete sense for him. He wanted to be able to walk into an elegant, ready-made space, full of distinctive character but not over-decorated. An oasis of modern comfort, fitted out for convenience. That's a fair description of today's perfect hotel.

The entire apartment is done in oaks and walnuts, used in a restrained way you would expect on a yacht. The two

different woods give the interior a very tailored, manly feeling, particularly in the sleek, ultrafunctional kitchen. Floor-to-ceiling cabinets and doors custom-clad in walnut veneer panels camouflage storage components. A Saarinen marble tulip table and dining chairs from Italy add the midcentury touch. Photo rails allow him to rotate his photography collection at will. Objects and decorative arts from all over Europe and Africa are also placed throughout the space.

The bedroom, done in a chocolate palette, is a completely masculine inner sanctum. A James Mont desk and chair make the room multifunctional; a pieced hide rug—one of his uniquely South American finds—adds pattern. In the bath, Fornasetti wallpaper provides humor and color. The living room ties all themes together: a gold sofa with embroidered pillows adds comfort, Paul McCobb chairs and a coffee table add savvy, and fashion memorabilia on the shelves add personality.

RIGHT: A James Mont desk in the bedroom is positioned for the view. PREVIOUS PAGES, 90: Circular and oval forms unite modern art and a traditional side table. PREVIOUS PAGES, 91: Dozens of eyes on Fornasetti wallpaper are meant to be humorously unnerving in the context of a bathroom. PREVIOUS PAGES: Simple art rails hold images by Bruce Weber, Craig McDean, and other fashion photographers. Kitchen cabinetry clad in walnut veneer helps it to blend with the rest of the furniture.

A Peruvian pieced-hide rug picked up in the course of travels adds a welcome burst of pattern into a tailored room that is dressed in calm shades of camel, other quiet neutrals, and tactile fur throws. The owner brought the Italian desk chair over from Italy.

HAUTE HOTEL When Starwood Hotels commissioned me to design the presidential suite at the St. Regis New York, the design directive was to make sure that the American and foreign dignitaries who use it regularly would feel as if they were arriving home when they came to stay. That's a diverse and exalted group, so it was a fantastic design challenge. And that wasn't all—Starwood also wanted to provide the captains of industry who use the suite for corporate meetings and out-of-office events with all the connectivity and technology of a modern boardroom. They explained that they were hiring our firm because we designed these same clients' private homes. That same level of design sensibility and detail was what these clients would expect from a home-away-from-home hotel suite.

The St. Regis is a New York icon of the Gilded Age—a high-style Beaux-Arts beauty built by John Jacob Astor IV. When it opened in 1904, it included all the latest conveniences, including butler service. Needless to say, its rooms have always been known for luxury, comfort, and handcrafted niceties. The hotel's general manager

is of the old school: he knows many of his clients by sight and remembers their individual preferences. He weighed in on our design at times in order to make sure that it would address their particular needs—and that it included the color gold, a favorite of one of the hotel's biggest clients.

It didn't surprise me that, when first I toured the existing suite, it was full of French art and antiques—the longtime mark of "good taste." I felt that as the presidential suite, though, it should represent American style. I decided to tuck some English influence into the French envelope to reflect our national heritage. As I sorted through samples and looked at various periods and styles, I kept asking myself: "What's French that could work in that vein? What's Anglo-inspired that makes sense? How can I bring the two together?" Napoleon III–style furnishings seemed the perfect solution. These nineteenth-century antiques are recognizable for their elegant gold-on-black detail, yet

RIGHT: The foyer introduces the suite's mélange of French, Anglo, and American decor with a parcel-gilt ebonized console in the style of Napoleon III, a Chippendale-influenced mirror, and classic black-and-white patterned marble floors.
OVERLEAF: Hand-embroidered wallpaper with a chinoiserie cherry blossom pattern on a deep, regal plum background covers the foyer's walls.

they're restrained enough to cross over into modern rooms and blend well with contemporary furnishings.

The foyer serves as prelude to the suite's entire symphony of detail. We begin by introducing a diamond-shaped motif that repeats throughout the suite, echoing the shape of the St. Regis's logo. Scenic wallpaper hand-embroidered with cherry blossoms on a regal plum background is a nod to tradition and luxury.

Camelback sofas in blush-colored velvet and high-back chairs covered in beige-and-white toile featuring a peacock motif make the living room truly inviting. The hotel made available its cache of unique and wonderful antiques to us, so we paired many of them—such as the commode in the dining room—with newer furnishings that shared a harmony of form. To make the library feel as if it were the guest's own, we paneled it in rich wood and stocked the shelves with travel books

To subtly reinforce the St. Regis brand, we echo the diamond shape of the hotel's iconic monogram throughout the suite. The motif reappears in various scales and incarnations in unexpected places: on grillwork, the fretwork backs of the dining chairs, the custom-embossed leather in the library, and the rug and bedding in the master bedroom.

French neoclassical touches that acknowledge the hotel's original style include symmetrically placed ornamental urns atop a fireplace mantel. Paired camelback sofas and high-back lounge chairs, however, add an element of Anglo-American design sensibility. The large mirror conceals a screen that works for professional A/V presentations as well as private television viewing.

and collectible objects you would be likely to have at home, such as antique globes, clocks, and Chinese jars.

The second bedroom is all about flexibility to accommodate different guests and different needs, so two full-size beds can stand separately or be pushed together to create a king. We had all of the bedclothes embroidered with another take on the diamond motif, and introduced Steuben glass and other pieces that recall our national heritage to give the room a definite American flavor.

In the master bedroom, the Napoleon III reappears. We had all the furniture, bedside tables included, custom made and fitted out to accommodate—and artfully hide—the necessary technology. We lined the bed with fabric woven of solid gold thread—a touch the hotel's best client will be sure to acknowledge—and topped it with a sumptuous baldachin fit for royalty.

RIGHT: Richly embroidered textiles and intricate trims speak to the hotel's legacy of fine artisanship. PREVIOUS PAGES: Travel-weary executives can relax in a cocoon of a paneled library, in which the rug's bold scale modernizes the Old-World atmosphere. PREVIOUS PAGES, 110–111: Our custom-designed bar cart perpetuates one of the hotel's great traditions: cocktail hour. OVERLEAF: Attention to details such as nailhead trim, and a rug and mirror that subtly reference the St. Regis's diamond-shaped logo sets the presidential suite apart. OVERLEAF, PAGE 118: The master bedroom features cloth spun of solid gold threads.

LA CASA EN EL CALLEJON As a child growing up in Colombia in the 1960s, my family's winter holidays were always spent in Cartagena. My memories have the magical quality of Slim Aarons's series *La Dolce Vita*: the historic walled city was crumbling at the time, yet it still had the romantic allure of Old Havana in the 1940s. So when a Swedish hotel concern invited me to fly to Cartagena five years ago and consult about converting a group of old houses into a boutique hotel, how could I refuse? Colombia is now having its moment and has finally become fashionable and chic, so they didn't have to ask me twice.

Many members of my family still have homes in Cartagena, and it's still a place where everyone who's lived there for an extended time knows everyone else, so I decided to try and travel under the radar since time was already short for the task at hand—this trip was not intended for social calls or distractions. After much perseverance and prodding, though, the client's

real estate agent discovered who I was. That's when she declared I needed a home of my own there—of course she said she had just the house for me. I reluctantly agreed to see it to appease her, but I made it clear that I wasn't in the market. On our way there she prepared me for the house's flaws, but then she divulged one major advantage: the current owner had altered the back of the courtyard house in the 1970s, so whoever purchased it had the freedom to make further changes. It could no longer be considered a landmarked property.

As we pulled up, a sad-looking sixteenth-century facade greeted us. The front door led to a dim, moldy foyer that in turn led to a giant but overgrown courtyard. As we explored, I became more and more amazed by things she apologized for or considered atrocities, like a water feature wall that was the coolest thing about the house.

LEFT: Fruit vendors, *palenqueras*, roam the city streets balancing bowls of fresh fruit on their heads and add even more color to street scenes. The style of this house's gated windows dates to the sixteenth century: exterior bars protect while jalousies on the interior adjust for privacy and light. PREVIOUS PAGES: Brilliant primary colors are everywhere in Cartagena, including on the facade of my cousin's house.

By the time we reached the roof terrace and took in its view of the Atlantic, I had become enchanted. I decided to buy the house on the spot. I would pay for that decision in more than money. The renovation of the house would become my Buddhist lesson. The differences in culture and design philosophy between this beautiful banana republic and New York would challenge everything I took for granted as a designer an architect, and a student of human nature—even though I had spent a significant part of my life there.

Typically, Cartagena's historic houses are a riot of color. Their pigmented plaster walls, each in a different hue, need regular refinishing. That was not for us. My vision was for a house designed like a chic, big-city boutique hotel: suited for lazy barefoot living, bathing suits, shorts during the day and sexy, elegant entertaining at night.

RIGHT: Sixteenth-century doors that lead to our house's interior courtyard still feature their original metal details. The foyer is the only space where I retained the color the previous owner had selected. American Gothic pews designed by Richard Upjohn come from the mid-ninteenth-century church that became the Limelight, in New York. PREVIOUS PAGES: Massive stone buttresses from the sixteenth-century Church of Santo Domingo loom opposite houses awash in the primary paints that color Cartagena.

We restored the 500-year-old ceiling to its original glory, *diente de perro* (dog's tooth) pattern and all. *Nichos*, or built-in wall lights, create a beautiful ambient glow in the evenings.
OVERLEAF, PAGE 135: Local artistic highlights include the Cathedral of San Pedro (second row, left; bottom row, center) and an exhibit by sculptor Sophia Vari (second row, far right).
OVERLEAF, PAGE 136–137: Tropical plants including banana leaves and birds of paradise freshen a blue-and-white dining area; the raw pottery is made locally.

130

I designed the entire house in four materials and four colors, all contrasted against white walls. After doing so much hotel work, it seemed practical to me to think of the bedrooms in terms of hotel sizing, too, so I followed a hospitality matrix for the bedrooms and designed one twin, one deluxe, a junior suite, and a king suite. All followed a similar model and used the same style of beds, doors, etc., as did the baths, which share the same line of fittings and fixtures to unify and simplify the look. I wanted the house to be as user-friendly as possible so that when my wife and I visited with friends instead of our children, they wouldn't feel like they were staying in our son's or daughter's room. Every bedroom features unique touches, but none projects a preordained "age." As with my hotel projects, differentiation comes from a chair, a bed fabric, or a dresser. That formulation simplifies life—and it's also

RIGHT: Lanterns I designed for Urban Electric fit well in the clean, whitewashed pool area. OVERLEAF: In the media room, a mix of white plaster, red doors, and chocolate-brown doorways reinterprets South American wall treatments and colors in a modern, chic way. Hernán Díaz's black-and-white photo from the 1960s captures the spirit of Cartagena. OVERLEAF, PAGE 144: A single bedroom just off the media room is dressed in vibrant blues and reds. OVERLEAF, PAGE 145: Vintage target tables add whimsy and fun. PREVIOUS PAGES: To experience this house—and Cartagena—is to feel the juxtaposition of old and new.

very Zen. Apart from our master suite, no one in our family has a dedicated room. If my daughter brings two friends and my son brings one friend, then my daughter stays in the room that transforms to three beds—the kids switch rooms every time we come.

The house's sixteenth-century section, the front-most part that faces the street, encompasses the entryway, *el zaguán*, and the living room. The ceiling was a masterpiece in dire need of tender-loving care. The carved beams were intact, and when freshly oiled, waxed, and painted they came to life again after almost five centuries—a real testament to their craftsmanship and quality. The living/dining room was freshened and modernized with plaster walls and a palette of ivories and complex neutrals. Pillows and art add bursts of vibrant color appropriate to the geographic location. As I selected

RIGHT: We updated the unique form of a circular stair, which had to remain in place, with a fresh coat of white paint. OVERLEAF: On the walls of the double bedroom, enlarged luggage stickers from all my favorite hotels—many of which I stayed in as a child—bring in wonderful, colorful graphics and a true if nostalgic sense of the romance of travel. PREVIOUS PAGES: Unique fabric patterns and lamps differentiate this guest room from others in the house that share the same general color scheme.

ABOVE: A terrace off the master bedroom offers great views of the city, particularly from the Jacuzzi tub. The textiles are from my own outdoor fabric collection. RIGHT: The master bath's glass-walled shower overlooks the city's historic rooftops.

the furnishings, I imagined the house belonging to a historic king's most trusted sea captain. The living room was his cabin, the place where he displayed his personal effects: the rosaries, the ubiquitous saints, portraits of the king and queen (today, Fornasetti plates), and gilded jewelry. Pre-Colombian pieces reference the country's ancient cultures. The Castiglioni light and other iconic twentieth-century pieces make the space relaxed and modern.

Combining the original dining room with the enormous kitchen gave me space to create a family/media room and an extra bedroom. The kitchen became a galley kitchen: clean, simple, and just as much counter space as we actually needed. The master suite takes up the entire third floor, with a bed whose headboard incorporates a desk on the reverse—again referencing the

LEFT: Paneled doors that line the master bedroom's walls come from the Palace of the Inquisition. Embroidered linens by Colombian Indians cover the bed. I designed the Brancusi-inspired table more than ten years ago, only to find that its slightly tribal form fits in well here, among pre-Colombian artifacts. The round mirror is from New England and continues the house's nautical theme. OVERLEAF: Paintings of traditional tall ships, hung in a modern arrangement, suit our master bedroom—a space I think of as a sea captain's cabin.

space-conscious designs of yachts or ships' cabins. The master bath is a little tropical fantasy, with teak benches and shower doors that open directly onto an exterior balcony. It boasts a view of the beautiful church of Santo Domingo, one of the city's most famous sites.

The rooftop features a simple open kitchen, and it's one of our favorite places to spend time. Early in the morning, wild parrots and toucans fill the trees, do fly-bys, and sometimes even eat off our plates. At sunset, when we sit looking out over the Atlantic Ocean and feeling the Santa Ana winds, we say to ourselves, *"¡Qué maravilla!"*

RIGHT: The rooftop terrace features an unexpected outdoor shower and a marvelous view of a historic cupola. The throw on the chaise is the kind of Colombian fabric typically used on a hammock. OVERLEAF: Colombia is home to the world's largest variety of indigenous fruits, which we try to sample as often as possible on our rooftop breakfast area. OVERLEAF, PAGES 162–163: A stunning view of the Atlantic Ocean—and of my aunt's yellow house a few streets over.

IT'S ALL IN THE MIX Personally as well as professionally, I'm both a designer and a collector. I love pieces from all different periods and cultures and I take great delight in blending big-ticket items with low-priced treasures in my own home as well as clients'. What matters to me is only that every piece in a room complements or sets off the pieces next to it. As long as things have the same *visual* value, they belong together. Pieces that have an affinity with each other—of form, color, or provenance—make the visual experience exhilarating. I say if it feels right, do it.

Rooms are works in progress. People always ask me if I fuss with the many things on display in my homes. Constantly. Arrangements should never be considered fixed for good. Each new acquisition will cause things to shift, relationships to change. As you rearrange what you already have to accommodate the new, remember to subtract occasionally as well. In a room with a true sense of collectedness, you feel that every single object, every single piece of furniture, was considered, acquired, placed, and rearranged over years and years, not just thrown together one day.

The success of an interior, for me, has to do with variety, sensibility, aesthetics, and craftsmanship—not price. Wonderfully handcrafted artistic pieces can give as much soul to a room as the finest antiques acquired at auction. Objects do not always have to be "real" to be lovely. For some projects, I even commission an artist I know who paints fabulous art "after the style of" famous artists. They are wonderful, affordable, and they give a room substantially the same vibe as an original. Any object that reveals mastery of some sort belongs at the bespoke level.

My feeling is: if you love it, live with it. This is an extraordinary time in design—beautiful things are available at every price point. If you collect, do so without fear. Never apologize for or try to explain a passion. Variety elevates the experience of the everyday—so mix it up.

SINCERELY YOURS How do you produce a space that is full of personality but still generally alluring enough to create a visceral attachment in a broad segment of the population? That's the challenge model apartments present. In real estate sales, design needs to be all things to all people—or to as many as possible. My solution is to cast a very wide net.

Experience has taught me that most of us want to live in a contemporary version of a traditional environment. We love to surround ourselves with familiar objects that connect us to the past. A piece from the house you grew up in—that's design comfort food. Adding an element of "now" comes from mixing expected elements with the new.

The entry is a study in restrained elegance. A black-and-white scheme is a simple design gesture that reads as a large one. The console, which matches the side tables in the living room, previews what's to come deeper inside the apartment. Atop it are ancient rings whose geometry plays off the straight bracers of the console's base and the curving sconces above. And nothing says "welcome" like a bountiful pot of peonies in peak bloom.

Here, the living room embraces everything from 1930s-inspired pieces to classic forms like a camelback sofa. Waylande Gregory's fabulous tabletop creations flash us back to the 1950s, and certainly look like they could have been handed down from one generation to the next. Oushak rugs are usually too traditional for me, but I decided they were right for this project as a traditional element, and I've since become crazy about them. Projects like this push me out of my comfort zone and regular design vocabulary, which is why I take them on whenever I can.

The dining room has a traditional sensibility, but white leather upholstery pulls dining chairs with a slightly Deco form into modernity. The botanical prints—plates purchased as a set in book form and framed individually—appeal to all nature lovers. They also introduce soft hints of color into an otherwise neutral palette.

Great design exists at every price point today, so why not take advantage of the available options? In the sunroom, metal coffee and end tables from Crate & Barrel sit

LEFT: White leather upholstery brings the silhouettes of dining chairs into bold relief. PREVIOUS PAGES: In a tailored-feeling living room, a restrained color palette makes for a very of-the-moment feel—and is sure to appeal to a broad audience. Wire-based side tables and a coffee table from Oly add modern nuance to custom-upholstered seating and a tableau of midcentury objects.

demurely next to bespoke upholstery. The high-low mi
is not apparent at all.

The master bedroom—done in a very pale shade of lavende
with glamorous burgundy accents—opens on one side to
wonderful planted terrace and on the other to an equall
spectacular bath. I'd never done a lavender room before
but it felt feminine, genteel, and charming—just what
wanted here. Interestingly, we found that it appealed to me
and women alike.

In the end, the building's developers sold the entire design—
lock, stock, and camelback sofa—not once, but *three* times
The first time they called and asked me to reproduce the
decor for a new buyer, I was flattered and happy to do it. By
the third time, I asked if we could possibly make it just a bi
different. We had to anyway, because somewhere along the
line I had picked up things that were one of a kind. That'
the designer in me.

RIGHT: The hip family room proves that it's possible to create a visually rich space without breaking the bank. The walls
look like they're covered in the preppiest of wallpaper, but they were simply made with innovation, a professional painter,
lots of tape, and a well-chosen color palette. Everything else we purchased at Room & Board: sofa, pillows, rug, art rail,
and frames. PREVIOUS PAGES, RIGHT: In the sunroom, comparatively cheap—but decidedly cheerful—was the rule for
artwork, side, and coffee tables. The high-back chair and the tailored sofa are investment pieces designed for longevity.

ABOVE: The bedroom's pale-as-a-whisper lavender walls enhance sunlight that floods in from a terrace and windows on the opposite wall. LEFT: A marble-lined bath always indicates luxury, and needs little embellishment besides interesting light fixtures and a silver cup full of fresh flowers.

DINNER AT EIGHT In 2009, Pamela Fiori, then the editor-in-chief of *Town & Country*, asked me to work with her on the magazine's apartment at the Hearst Designer Vision Showcase. That year, the theme was Hollywood movies—great for inspiration. Because the economy had just come to a screeching halt, she thought *Dinner at Eight*—George Cukor's 1933 comedy of manners—would strike a timely tone. Clearly, the interior of the duplex we drew had to include more ideas people could try at home than inaccessible, aspirational objects with hefty price tags.

I based the downstairs on the Jordan family, the movie's old-money clan whose shipping business the Depression hit hard. Upstairs I channeled Kitty Packard, the gold-digging bride of a nouveau-riche mining magnate. On the first floor, we devised a wall treatment—with a little creative taping and a very light cement-colored paint—that resembled the interior of the Jordans' on-screen house. Once the tape was peeled up, voilà: elegant limestone. (That was the first tip.)

The entryways include items that feel handcrafted—vases, bowls, a whimsical Calder piece that is actually a museum-shop reproduction. (That was lesson number two: not everything has to be an artist's original, or even authentic.)

ABOVE: Reproduction side tables of a Jean-Michel Frank design for the Rockefellers begin the trope of what the Jordans' interior style might have looked like. OVERLEAF: The living room's high/low mix includes table lamps from Crate & Barrel and traditional sconces featuring crystal and parcel gilt. The contemporary Arbus-style credenza has Bérard-inspired, hand-painted molding and whimsical amethyst pulls.

Create an environment that you love by bringing in things you love, regardless of their origins. We also reimagined the commode: it had an eighteenth-century form, but we painted it to achieve a Christian Bérard feeling and added amethyst pulls. (Lesson three: it's possible to find a humble piece in a vintage shop and make it look like much, much more.)

The living room feels at once traditional and modern thanks to clean, simple lines and a beige-and-ivory palette. Color enters the room through artwork, an Aubusson rug—a traditional piece that the Jordans might well have owned—and the foyer's hand-embroidered scenic wallpaper. The lacquer table infuses the room with an Asian undertone very popular in the 1930s.

We pay tribute to the golden days of Hollywood in the loft-like dining room. We reinvented the room in the spirit of set-designer-turned-interior-designer Tony Duquette, whose ornate and whimsical chandelier hangs enchantingly over the table. To break up the space, we found a comparatively inexpensive screen that we dressed up on one side with malachite-patterned wallpaper, with mirror on the other.

RIGHT: A silver cocktail set and Lalique crystal glasses and decanters rest on an unexpected Lucite tray. OVERLEAF: A black-and-white home office doesn't age. FOLLOWING PAGES, 190: Hand-painted faux limestone walls recall the Jordan family's magnificent on-screen home. PREVIOUS PAGES: With its Tony Duquette light fixture, bold patterns, and malachite-papered screen, the dining room is an homage to my dear friend Hutton Wilkinson. We spruced up the enticing-but-affordable console with malachite pulls.

RAUSCHENBERG ART AND LIFE NEW EDITION MARY LYNN KOTZ

Cézanne in Provence

THOMAS EAKINS   YALE UNIVERSITY PRE

THE GREAT MASTERS

THE MUSÉE D'ORSAY

STEPAN & HAHNER **SPIRITS SPEAK** A CELEBRATION OF AFRICAN MASKS ★ PRESTEL

DOMINIQUE BROWNING THE NEW GARDEN PARADISE

conran CHINESE STYLE the art of living   BRADLEY QUINN

I WANT TO SPEND THE REST OF MY LIFE EVERYWHERE, WITH EVERYONE, ONE TO ONE, ALWAYS, FOREVER, NOW.   DAMIEN HIRST

UNDER WORLD   KELLY KLEIN

(Lesson four: high style and glamour can be attainable

modern, and new.)

The sunroom/sitting room/home office—people today wan

multifunction spaces—is designed for family members of al

ages. The Buddha and the gold-and-black fans I found i

Chinatown for next to nothing. They're fun and attain th

Zen vibe I was hoping for.

The boudoir is purposely over the top to the point of kitsch t

reflect Kitty's gold-digging taste—inevitable clashy zebra ru

included—but people still took away some real decoratin

ideas. The walls again showed off the magic of paint: a pale

blue background and metallic silver diamond grid gave th

small room the illusion of depth and a shimmery 1930s quality

The allure of the seemingly unattainable always makes a spac

memorable. The issue lies in how we define that term. Fo

me, it means the handcrafted, the artisanal, the one-of-a-kind

Irreplaceable and unique things make life rich, so we scattere

plenty of them throughout. (Lesson five, exit stage left.)

PREVIOUS PAGES: To reflect Kitty Packard's social climbing aspirations, we created a collage of celebrity photographs on
"her" bedroom wall. Contrary to expectation, the light walls with metallic diamond patterning make the room feel larger.
FOLLOWING PAGES: The sunroom and terrace offer New York's greatest luxury: outdoor space. Urban Archeology loaned
the lamp posts, which once stood in front of One Wall Street—just where Mr. Jordan's office would have been.

OVER THE TOP I believe that family and friends are the key ingredients of a well-lived life. The couple who owns this home does, too, and that's what I most love about them. When we met, they had just purchased two magnificent duplex penthouse apartments in one of Lower Manhattan's most prestigious buildings. We planned a total architectural overhaul to combine the two units, and our common goal was to create a glamorous front-of-house for adults and entertaining, a hip, club-like family room, five comfortable bedrooms for their children and a nanny, an elegant study for him, plus an ultra-alluring master suite.

Reconfiguring the entry to suit their vision—and the grandeur of the space's palatial 12-foot ceilings—required that we replace the existing stair with a sinuous, floating version. Clad in Macassar ebony and carpeted in a blue silk leopard print, it now provides a highly dramatic first glimpse of the apartment. We encased the entry walls in intricately carved limestone, cut and pieced to resemble an ultramodern basketweave—a true design feat that

involved establishing the overall rhythm and composition on paper, then numbering each piece before setting a single stone. The result is nothing short of spectacular, if I do say so myself. A palazzo floor in limestone, wood and stainless steel adds the final visual delight.

The double-height living room is dressed in a delicate-yet-vibrant palette of blue and purple accents. Artwork by Russian master painters adds depth to the already richly detailed environment. The dining room, fittingly, is all about bounty. It's configured to seat fourteen guests—at a minimum—and its table divides in half to accommodate double that number for the holidays.

Without physically dividing the original kitchen, we split the space into two distinct areas. One side is a bright space for family dining, lined in lime green and white—it just radiates pure joy. At the opposite end of the space, zebra-wood-faced cabinets and restaurant-grade appliances

RIGHT: The Macassar-clad circular stair and walls of limestone cut to resemble woven ribbon are both feats of engineering as much as design. OVERLEAF: Silver damask curtains in a moiré pattern and textured walls bring warmth to the palatial, double-height living room. PREVIOUS PAGES: Double-height terraces provide spectacular views of Lower Manhattan. The glass barriers create a functional windscreen that allowed a garden to be set up at penthouse level.

provide every amenity the family's personal chef could request. Its white, Parsons-style counter and Lucite-and-chrome bar stools, make it feel like a chic dining venue a few blocks north, in SoHo.

The way the clients described what they wanted in the master suite and bath at first sounded to me like a series of oxymorons that I thought were unachievable: "Elegantly laid back." "Sensually Zenlike." "Comfortably opulent." Looking back now, at the end of the project, I laugh because much to my surprise, those descriptions really do fit the playfully swank rooms we designed for this youthful, much-in-love couple's private retreat. The poignant views from the bedroom make me think of a favorite movie from 1970: *On a Clear Day You Can See Forever*, starring Barbra Streisand and Yves Montand. The windows also look toward the World Trade Center, a wonderful reminder that resilience and courage are not only possible but a way of life—these two are living proof of that.

PREVIOUS PAGES: These clients love to spend time with family and friends, so we created a dining room that is all about abundance and conviviality. The table splits into two for large parties; as arranged for everyday use, it seats fourteen; when separated, the number almost doubles. The Venetian marble floors, the Italian faience amphora atop the Macassar console, and the mercury-glass chandelier combine elements of old and new.

ABOVE: His office features the detailing and atmosphere typical of Old-World elegance, but the highly polished woods and a two-tone color scheme bestow modern sophistication and luxuries. RIGHT: A powder room subverts traditional aesthetics while maintaining quality craftsmanship found in historic homes. Its patterned walls, brilliant color, and play of textures keep it youthful, hip, and chic.

Areas differentiated by color palette and style of furnishings help to divide an outsized kitchen into two distinct spaces. To the left is the area for casual family dining. Above is a kitchen fitted out for a personal chef and for sophisticated soirées with friends.

We designed the children's rooms as if they were yach interiors with not an inch to spare. Built-ins always make the best use of space, and teens find them hip because they can customize the contents of the shelves and nooks. The eldest boy wanted the color scheme of his room modeled after his father's favorite Ferrari: black, yellow, and chrome The second eldest chose black, red, and chrome—clearly another Ferrari, and a Grand Prix winner.

The double-height terrace space provides a garden in the sky. The views from them are nothing short of breathtaking: you can see from the Statue of Liberty to the Brooklyn Bridge and everything in between. Moc outdoor furniture encourages guests to delight in the views and in the warm summer breezes, and to bask in the glow of good company.

Even though this New York residence is quite expansive overall, space is still at a premium in the children's bedrooms. To make the best use of every available square inch, in a son's bedroom we created vertical storage space by building in a case piece that is actually a finely calibrated example of modern interior architecture.

RIGHT: This couple is youthful and successful, and their bedroom reflects those facts. A high-roller style retreat full of fun and color suits them well—and yes, it's also a little bit wild.
OVERLEAF: A 1960s-inspired, quasi-Gucci link pattern in gold tile makes the master bath a cross between Lil' Kim and Jackie O.

214

THE EVOLVING HOUSE A home needs to evolve. The question I'm asked most often is: "Do you change everything in your home all the time?" I do, but not for the reasons that most people would suppose. In the fifteen years since my wife and I built our house in Sagaponack, its transformation has continued to surprise and delight me. From the beginning it has been a family house. We do not entertain much in the city, so for summers and holiday weekends we wanted a welcoming, always-room-for-another-at-the-table kind of place.

The predictable phases of family life lead to seismic shifts in decoration. Our living room, library, and dining room were once exclusively grown-up areas. The family room and covered porch were a place for the kids to play with friends. Fast forward nineteen years, when my son pointed out that his room still looked like it had when he was a toddler. I was devastated. His room was so cute! The concept for it came out of my own childhood. My siblings had learned to pilot planes when we were growing up in Florida, and covered their walls with beautiful blue flight maps. I found a company that made giant maps and hung them on my son's bedroom walls. We bought model airplanes and hung them from the ceiling, which we had painted to resemble clouds. The addition of an Italian ceiling fixture that looked like a UFO made my son feel as if that room was the center of the universe. We eventually redid his room in a more sophisticated tone. He said he wanted lots of artwork, which was music to my ears. I immediately thought of all the fantastic pieces I had in storage—where better to place them than in his room for him to enjoy?

That room was only the beginning. We changed the family room to something teens would actually use. Then, we realized, the covered porch had to change too. And so on. Change happens for a reason. So yes, in the end, I do change things constantly—but mainly to keep up with the times.

HOME IS WHERE THE ART IS Family life evolves over time—parents are often loathe to contemplate that fact, but it's true. Our country house, which we built fifteen years ago, is a perfect example of that. In my first book, *Modern Luxury*, the house is presented as it looked when our children were young. Now they're already both in college. The rooms have changed to reflect this development and our needs—and my ever-growing, ever-shifting collections.

Off the bat, the entry tells a story about how taste changes over time. Here's just one aspect of it. About seven years ago, my son formed a collection of limited edition, artist-designed toys from Kidrobot. KAWS, then just becoming a name, was one of the Kidrobot artists, so my son became familiar with his work and decided to give me a real KAWS piece for my birthday that year. He and his mother found me a small stainless-steel sculpture that's on the hall table in our city apartment. A painting from KAWS's cartoon series

LEFT: The foyer tells the story of our family interests in layers upon layers of art and objects, including a grouping of surfboards that seems appropriate for a summer getaway in the Hamptons.
PREVIOUS PAGES: In a collector's life, amalgamation and serendipity play essential roles in what's placed where.

223

A color explosion created by a Calder gouache and one of Niki de Saint Phalle's *Nana* sculptures balances the brilliant red introduced by the longboard. The Danish stove adds my favorite color combination: blue and white. OVERLEAF, LEFT: A stack of books by Korean artist Airan Kang reflects off the mirrored-glass surfaces of Rob Wynne's mushrooms. OVERLEAF, RIGHT: A bowl of vintage billiard balls atop a Boulle cabinet suggests our family's fun-loving nature.

FOLLOWING PAGES, 228–229: My wife, Marcia, is a passionate nature lover so she fell for this multimedia piece by Timothy John Berg and Rebekah Myers. David Salle's portrait of Marcia, obviously very dear to me, entices guests into a corner of the living room beyond the stair. FOLLOWING PAGES, 230: A sixteenth-century Gothic table and a chair by Claude Lalanne shows that all good pieces *do* go together.

224

very cloud has a silver linin

came next. Later, I saw one of his sculptures at a gallery in L.A. and decided that I had to have one like it . . . but I purchased it over the Internet, thinking it was about 4 feet tall and not paying attention to the actual dimensions. I waited months for it to be made. It was eventually delivered—all II feet of it. I started to think about where I was going to put it and while I did, I leaned it up against the entry wall. When we next came out to the house, we felt it looked perfect exactly where I had left it. It welcomes everyone who comes in and immediately puts a big smile on their face.

The living room demonstrates how the introduction of a new piece can transform everything else around it, particularly when each individual piece is extraordinary. Mattia Bonetti's Chewing Gum table, which I pursued for years, eventually replaced a much more traditional table. Its visual mate at the other end of the sofa is by

RIGHT: Even a drawing by Niki de Saint Phalle features curves as a major motif, like her larger-than-life sculptures. OVERLEAF: My wife and I truly enjoy creating crazy, colorful, unexpected tablescapes. The Tony Duquette chandelier is a great inspiration. PREVIOUS PAGES: I practice what I preach about there being no rules. A Ruhlmann table sits to one side of the sofa; Mattias Bonetti's Chewing Gum table cozies up to the other. A motif of repeated curves bring the room's disparate elements together.

Ruhlmann. The two couldn't be more different in form or origin, but they look wonderful together because of their similarly arched legs. The Lalanne table came much later. The sixteenth-century Gothic table then became a backdrop for artful arrangements.

The dining room, however, charts the true arc of our evolutionary timeline as a family. When I purchased its Gothic windows from the Tacoma Museum in Washington at auction, the house was under construction. As a young designer, I thought good rooms had themes, so I did Gothic here, Gothic there, Gothic everywhere around the house. Very soon afterward, we realized that all that Gothic didn't fit with our life. Enter the two Tony Duquette twig chandeliers, which I purchased at a Christie's sale in Los Angeles. Subsequently, many more pieces of his entered the mix.

RIGHT AND OVERLEAF: The family dining area off the kitchen used to be a playful explosion of mixed colors and mismatched patterns aimed at young children. PREVIOUS PAGES 238–239: A guest bedroom before and after my most recent makeover of the house. PAGES 240–241: My son's bedroom as it was through his childhood, at left, and as it is now. The change was necessary to grow with him, but it is still a bit bittersweet.

I am obsessed with blue—and especially blue in combination with white. For many years, our kitchen was finished in an unusual, gorgeous blue strié with a thick glaze. For us, it was the ultimate country kitchen.

When I redid the kitchen recently, I decided to make everything that had once been blue, white—and vice versa. The paint finish is the same, heavily glazed strié, just in a different color, so the kitchen—chic as it now is— still has a heartwarming modern-meets-Old-World feeling.

For years, we thought our kitchen was the ultimate country kitchen. It was painted in a gorgeous blue strié with a very thick glaze. The chairs were mismatched and multi-colored, which made for a playful room— great for the kids. Not long ago, I updated the space: what was white is now blue; what was blue, white. It's all done in the same strié, however. Modern chairs and white counters make the room much cleaner and sophisticated. We were ready to be done with juvenile touches for a while.

People constantly ask me if I change my houses all the time. I do. I am fascinated by the serendipity of how and why things come together. I am affected by the changes brought about by time. Staying dynamic, cool, and current for me is where the fun is.

RIGHT: Our recently redesigned casual dining area feels just right for a family that is now grown up. OVERLEAF: I carried the blue-and-white palette into the adjacent family room. FOLLOWING PAGES, 254–255: Yes, I am obsessed with the room's color scheme—right down to the backgammon set and accent pieces. FOLLOWING PAGES, 256–257: In the summer, our screen porch becomes the most-used room in the house. Lucy, queen of the roost, lounges on a sofa covered in a fabric I designed for Stark.

PREVIOUS PAGES AND LEFT: A beautifully set table will always make guests feel welcome and appreciated. OVERLEAF, LEFT: The view from our dock. OVERLEAF, RIGHT AND 262–265: Because Marcia works with the Central Park Conservancy, she was able to commission the gentleman who created the park's rustic playground to build our pergola. It quickly became our favorite outdoor dining spot. Marcia created the intensely English gardens that surround it.

259

I dedicate this book to Marcia, Nicholas and Alexandra
who have inspired me to be at my best at all times.
They have done so by being an example of everything I admire.

ACKNOWLEDGMENTS Lilian Mishaan, Jeffrey Simpson,
Douglas Benach, Margaret Russell, Michael Boodro,
Pamela Fiori, Carlos Mota, Anita Sarsidi,
Fiona Waterstreet, John Alexander, Symon and Elina Garber,
George Ross, Joshua McHugh, Roger Davies,
Francesco Lagnese, Douglas Friedman, Massimo Listri,
Marco Ricca, Thomas Loof and Trevor Tondro.

PHOTOGRAPHY CREDITS

Roger Davies: 124, 126, 127, 129, 130–31, 132, 133, 134, 135, 136–37, 138, 139, 141, 142–43, 144, 145, 146–47, 149, 150–51, 152, 153, 154, 156–57, 159, 160, 161, 162–63

Douglas Friedman: 123, 199, 201, 202–3, 204, 205, 207, 208, 209, 210, 211, 212, 213, 214–15, 216, 217

Douglas Friedman/Trunk Archive: 87, 91, 96–97

Francesco Lagnese: 179, 180, 181, 182, 183, 184, 185, 186, 187, 188, 189, 190, 191, 192, 193, 195, 196, 197, 220, 222–23, 230, 231, 235, 239, 241, 251, 252–53, 254, 255, 256–57, 258–59, 261, 262–63, 264, 265, 266, 267, 268–69, 270

Massimo Listri: 224–25, 226, 228, 229, 232–33, 236, 237, 238, 243, 244–45, 246–47, 248–49

Thomas Loof/Trunk Archive: 88–89, 90, 92, 93, 95

Joshua McHugh: 5, 6, 33, 36–37, 39, 44, 45, 46, 47, 49, 50, 51, 52, 61, 62–63, 64, 66–67, 68–69, 70, 71, 72–73, 75, 76, 77, 79, 80–81, 82, 83

Jessica Nash: 30–31

Marco Ricca: 11, 55, 56–57, 58, 59, 227, 240

George Ross Photographs, Inc.: 2, 15, 16–17, 18, 20, 21, 22, 25, 26–27, 28, 29, 35, 40, 41, 42, 43, 99, 101, 102, 103, 104, 105, 106–7, 108, 109, 110, 112, 113, 115, 116, 117, 118, 119, 120–21, 167, 168–69, 170, 172, 173

Trevor Tondro: 23

Library of Congress Control Number: 2014943615

Printed in China

Design by Doug Turshen with Steve Turner

www.monacellipress.com

10 9 8 7 6 5 4 3 2 1
First edition